WE ARE

Lisa Kanemoto

Introduction by Morrie Camhi

Outreach Press
P.O. Box 29026
San Francisco, CA 94129

ISBN 0-9613699-0-6
Library of Congress Catalog Card Number 84-90606

Designed and produced by Lisa Kanemoto

Typography by Custom Typography Service
Printed in the U.S.A. by Phelps Schaefer

for Mary Dunlap
whose love of justice extends to all

Introduction

Among those things I don't know is the answer to a persistent question.

Why are humanist photographers consistently given less attention by galleries, muse-ums, collectors and publishers?

It seems inconsistent with our own definition "as humans" for this to be so. No fundamental concern for our species will be forthcoming if we do not provide it for ourselves. After a lifetime of philosophic inquiry and construction, Jean Paul Sartre announced his deathbed discovery: *the meaning of life is our experience of each other.*

Humanism is certainly centered on human nature and activity. But there is a small undercurrent of additional meaning that filters into the word. It is the implication that one of the important things we do, as humans, is to architect *ideals.*

There have been waves of pessimism in the photography of people. The photographer's preoccupation has centered on the unfortunate, the impoverished, the unscrupulous, the brutal, the ugly or the bizarre. Even those photographers concerned with social commen-tary often reduce their subjects to the cliché of the pathetic.

A small minority of positivism has persisted. These are photographers who would "rather light a candle than curse the darkness." There is the impish hedonism of Lartigue, the understated embrace of Alinder's America, the poetic shadow-people of De Carava or the partisan handshake of Dotter.

There are too few others.

Now, added to this small group, is Lisa Kanemoto's heartfelt, totally open and accepting look at the homosexual community.

Her subjects apparently trust her presence. They respond to her camera with naturalness.

For a subject so often treated sensationally, with exploitation, with preordained scenarios of myth or forbidden fantasy—Kanemoto's approach is refreshing.

The photographs are neither pretentious nor erudite.

We meet these people as Lisa Kanemoto does, in the common manner of day-to-day life. They share themselves *twice:* once through the observations of Kanemoto's camera and again when they write for us on the facing page.

For those who have already been determined to know this important, dynamic section of our society, there are probably no new discoveries or insights in the Kanemoto essay.

This does not diminish its importance. Anyone who has purchased a case of wine has voted for the value of repeated savorings. Is the second bottle diminished merely because it wasn't the first?

Today, more than ever, warm embraces need repeating.

MORRIE CAMHI

Habit-clad, hips swaying, attention-seeking, Fred Brungard, "Sister Missionary Position," inspired my interest in gay people. I judged him severely as weird and frivolous. Yet I photographed him with fascination and discovered a most sensitive, thoughtful man with the unusual courage to act out what he believes in, and I felt ashamed of my prejudices.

Sincere thanks to each person portrayed here for trusting me, for enriching my life with their individual qualities and for having been so disarmingly open and kind.

A special thanks to Morrie Camhi, who with photography opened a new world for me, to Thomas Waddell for believing in this project, to my husband, children and friends for their support and encouragement.

My gratitude to the National Endowment for the Arts.

LISA KANEMOTO

In the world I work and long for
Women do not get wounded
For being women.
And men do not fight wars
For being men.
Color does not clash with color.
Every color is beautiful, necessary
In its relation to every other.

Dream on, scoff the cynics, dream on.

In the world I am in now
I am one infinitesimal speck of life,
A lesbian woman dreamer advocate life
Who believes it possible
For this world to be more and more
The one I work and long for.

And in the dream world
There is never too much loving between women,
There is never too much loving between men,
And wrong ways of touching
Are intimately discovered
And intimately changed
In care for the person touched.
The hand of the law does not seize or strike
Me, or anyone, for who we love.
Homophobes embrace lesbians.
Fag-baiters, fag-bashers reach out to gay men
As people.
Lesbians, gay men, forgive, comprehend, hug back
And the cynics learn to swim
In tears of joy.

MARY C. DUNLAP

All I ever wanted was *my* life.

Dana Sanders, Secretary

Why do people who react negatively or with disbelief toward my sexuality think that I could as easily "go straight" and be happier? Why do they think I want to change or love someone that is not natural for me to love? I'm happy loving women.

My sex life is a small part of my life, a facet of my whole being. With people who cannot accept it, it becomes an exaggerated issue.

But I try not to let anyone else's opinion of gay people affect my happiness. I am secure and happy with at least this part of my life, my lovers and friends.

MELISSA REICHARD, Artist
CRYSTAL LANG, Photographer

At a very early age I was aware of being gay. It was very difficult to be open about my sexual preference living on an Indian reservation and being proud of my Paiute heritage. Now that I am out, I hope to be a positive role model for young Gay American Youths.

RANDY T. BURNS, Secretary

We have lived happily together for eight years. Rick's name was changed to Baggett after our Holy Union Ceremony in Nashville, Tennessee, our hometown. In San Francisco we do not have to hide the fact that we are gay.

RAYMON BAGGETT, Designer
RICK BAGGETT, Chef

Since womanlove is one of the most beautiful, joyous forces in my life, and I am proud of it, I hesitated to come out to my parents only because I was afraid I might somehow disappoint them. But instead they responded with understanding and acceptance. Both my parents have always supported whatever was right for me. Their love and faith in me have nurtured inestimably my confidence and strength.

CYNTHIA HUSSEY, Music Student

Carly has two moms. Our family is a circle of variety and dependability. We are in love.

Lesbian Family: SLEAZY, Machinist
CATHY CADE, Photographer, Mother, Housecleaner; and son CARLY

I had always felt and known that I was really meant to be a woman. Every day, every hour I experience discrimination. But I keep my head high and walk straight. I am proud to be a transsexual.

ELISSA LORRAINE, Telephone Operator

One is put on this earth with obstacles to go through. I try to conquer them and live life to the fullest.

TOM SOUZA, Model

I have always been attracted to the masculine. Not until I met and fell in love with a masculine woman, did I know the full fruition of my attraction.

DEBI SUNDAHL, Erotic Dancer
NAN KINNEY, Construction Worker

To my first woman lover, thank you, thank you, thank you.

SHIRLEY WILSON, Nurse

In 1970 I was 19, gay and a medic with the Marines in Vietnam. The pain of seeing men, beautiful men I loved, destroyed is still with me. These men live in my dreams and stride through my fantasies. We must never allow another war to waste our brothers and sisters.

MIKE FELKER, Veterans Certification Supervisor

About my homosexuality—I feel privileged. Sometimes I think I'm experiencing twice as much living as others who have not liberated themselves. Soon, perhaps, we can drop the labels, when we all realize that sexuality is not black and white, but a marvelous nuance.

DR. THOMAS F. WADDELL, Physician
ZOHN ARTMAN

I don't feel either way about gayness. Life itself is enough. Just like being black: I am not responsible for my color or sexuality.

SYLVESTER, Singer

S&M has to do with a mutually agreed-upon exchange of power in which the slave voluntarily subjects himself to his master's will. In brief, Michel has found his freedom in slavery to the man he loves, and similarly, Charles has found his in the possession this involves.

CHARLES M. DURHAM, Social Worker
MICHEL DE LA ROCHE, Tour Director

My puppet characters always expressed androgyny, even before my own sexuality developed. As my art evolved, I became one of my androgynous beings. I have experienced conception, birth, meditation, rebirth and death with my puppet children and attribute this to the androgynous intimacy we share.

GABRIEL TULLE, Puppeteer

I had a lot of difficulties in the Navy when they found out I was gay. I felt very pressured and had to go through many legal battles.

J. T., Counselor

Never again!

EDUARDO SOTO, Store Manager

I never chose to love men. I love the way that has always felt right to me.

If today somebody gave me the choice to be either straight or gay, I'd choose to be straight. It would be an easier life.

MARK BRYANT, Photo Instructor

Being gay around my Indian people is like being a green-colored fish in a pond of other green fish. I feel my people acknowledge me as a person, as family.

ERNA PAHE, President, American Indian Club; and daughter SHANNAN

I am on an ever unending circular quest to discover those aspects of myself unrecognized, unwanted and beyond gender identification. I do not see drag or make-up as disguise, but rather as clues to the discovery of hidden souls and characters held within.

AGNES DE GARRON, Choreographer/Director

I take my calling as a rabbi, psychologist and pastoral counselor with great seriousness. It was necessary for me to undergo treatment and full psychoanalysis to adjust to marriage and children. The psychoanalytic process continued to enable me to adjust to what was my lifestyle. My belief in a creator gave me my key: for as his creation, my desires and needs could be perceived and are natural. Thus I can live honestly as a gay person.

DR. BENJAMIN MARCUS, Rabbi

Being a strong aggressive woman, Jewish and Gay, has not been a major asset in my past.

At age 16, when I was just coming out, I was led to believe that a family consisted only of blood relations. That wasn't enough support for me, so I proceeded to challenge it— and a lot of the other ideals set forth by society. In creating a new lifestyle for myself and others, I have found many different options: I opened the Artemis Cafe; I was co-founder, with a women's bookstore, of a women's community; and now I am a mother. I love being a woman. I love being in love. Having a family of both gay and straight men and women has been a dream fantasy of mine all my life.

SARA LEWINSTEIN, Restaurant Owner

Freedom is never lost; it is given up, relinquished or simply dies of disuse.

BILL GRAHAM, Meditation Teacher

My difficulties and heartaches of growing up in Kansas as a gay person have become a distant memory. Living here in San Francisco among so many gay people who accept themselves has been a healing experience. In my search to understand and make peace with myself, I discovered my own deeply spiritual nature. Out of this I learned to fully accept and love myself.

JON HARRIS, Artist

We are a Papa, a Daddy and a son. Growing is part of our daily routine. It's hard work being a family with commitments to raising ourselves. Parenting is full of joys and pains—sharing and caring—teaching and learning—cries and laughter. All of this makes us proud of the family we are.

Maybe someday there will be a sister for Bryce.

MERIT CHARLES, Teacher
BILL PHILIPS, Computer Analyst; and son BRYCE

When I consider the many different ways in which human beings live: single, married, cooperatively on the street . . . being lesbian/gay is like one of the ripples on a pond.

It's important to make choices that will satisfy and complement our being and those around us.

The choices I have made so far in my life are allowing me to be quite happy.

DEBORAH MATTHEWS, Mother, Fashion Consultant

Man is sexual. The finite—hetero, bi, homo, non—are simply man's need to make order out of chaos. I love my brothers and sisters.

BEN HERNANDEZ, Medical Researcher

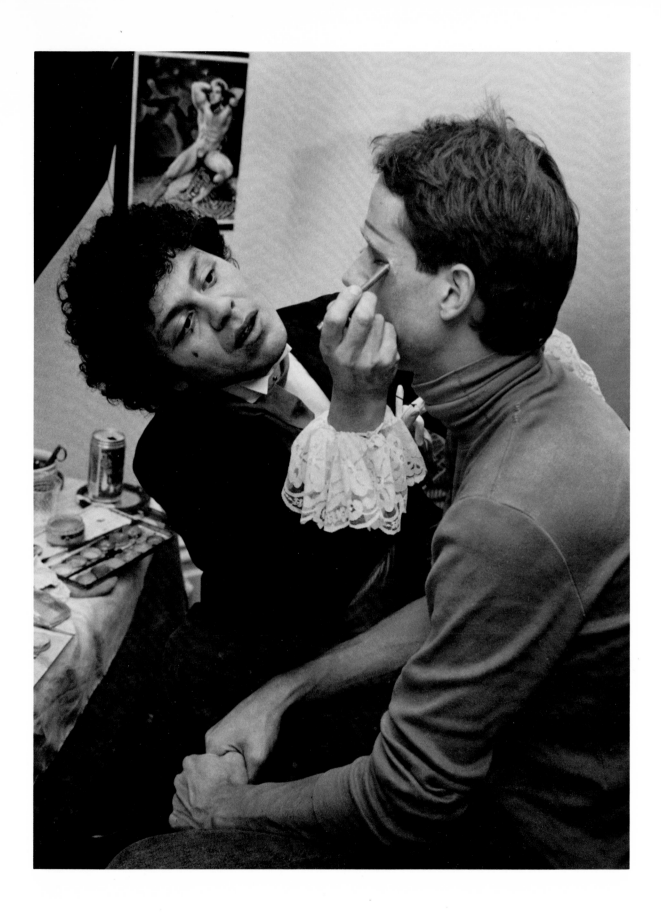

—

When I realized my homosexuality—admitted it and lived it—I no longer had to deal with guilt and loneliness. I found understanding, acceptance and family.

JOHN ORTIZ CLAS, Bar Manager

Being a radical lesbian feminist when I first came out provided me with a foundation from then on for understanding the world and its forces in political terms. Political consciousness and organizing skill are things they can never take away. As long as our brains are intact, we will have the skill to view what's going on around us; we'll know how to think and assess and organize. Women, gays, communities of color, poor people— we'll challenge what we think is unfair or not working. That is why we're seen as a threat.

CANYON SAM, Poet, Editor, Electrician

I discovered that in taking risks, I somehow managed to be a role model for another. It is terrifying to take a risk, but it is even more terrifying not to. At least I know that I have directly participated in controlling a part of my life.

BERNICE SOOHOO LEE, Executive Director,
Association for Children's Rights and Services

Since childhood I have loved costumes and dressing up. I feel it has nothing to do with my being gay; rather, it is an expression of happiness in one of its many signatures.

MICHAEL JOHNSTON, Telephone Operator
JON HARRIS

Being gay? It's the same as having blue eyes or gray hair. It's all part of a bigger whole. When I'm asked to think about it, though, there is no doubt it has been a gift in so many ways. I've had to learn about prejudice, love, the church; my life has meant a much closer examination of life process for all people because of my gayness. I would hate to think anyone's sexuality was the ruling factor. The real issue for me, or anyone, is their spirituality, not their sexuality.

ZOHN ARTMAN, Publicist

For me as a gay man to be part of our culture in a significant way is the fulfillment of a dream come true.

JAMES H. MC CLURE, Deputy Sheriff

"And together we re-create each other." (Kaddish Symphony. From Kabbalistic literature)

Lovers

I don't know why one person is straight and another is gay. What I do know is that love has no gender.

DEAN STEINER, Art Director

Those who are full of resentment have a harder adjustment to make.

GENIE M. MC AFEE, Telephone Craft Person; and son KEN

At an early age I heard the call to the religious life. When I was 12 I entered a Capuchin seminary intending to become a Franciscan priest. Confronting my gay desires at 19, I heeded my spiritual director's advice and returned to "the world," half believing the "heterosexual adjustment" he counseled would be possible. While attempts were made, the truth of my life was triumphant. By age 24 I had fully embraced my gayness, and by 34 I had rediscovered my vocation to the religious life—not, however, as a Franciscan priest but as a gay male nun in the city of St. Francis.

FRED BRUNGARD, Sister Missionary Position

I believe that being a lesbian or gay man, in this world, can be transformed into blessings, curses or nothing. Aren't there actually many more than two sexes, as many as there are chemical elements or flowers, and more to be discovered? I know that I have been several distinct sexes in my lifetime so far; in this, I am hardly unusual. But, to *enjoy* the changes in oneself and others—now, that *is* unusual.

We must preserve our diversity by thriving on it, conquering the fear of differences that leads to killing off animals, sexes, ideas in favor of predictable pairs. I shout Hooray! that in our lifetimes we have come out in great and colorful numbers, and are busy loving and learning to love better.

MARY C. DUNLAP, Civil Rights Lawyer

Cover:

Quiet submission. Please pass me by.
                KEN BUNCH, Investigator

Opposite Title Page:

Political work keeps me from being angrier; a spiritual path is necessary to my survival; women's crafts, whether painting or quilting, move me to my core; I do not want separatism. I wish to see gay and straight people united.
                FRANCESCA DUBIE, Musician, Producer, Teacher, Psychic

Back Cover:

I am a woman, I am a Lesbian. I can't compromise myself just to please others. I have to be who I am.
                CATHY CORTEZ

Being gay is living true to myself; a model to explore and express other truths in my life.
                KITTY TSUI, Author of The Words of a Woman Who Breeds Fire

DANA SANDERS, GABRIEL TULLE, MARK BRYANT, RANDY BURNS

LISA KANEMOTO, *formerly a goldsmith from Germany, lives in San Francisco, where she works as a free-lance photographer. She has produced several photo essays, including series on multi-handicapped youths, Chinese immigrants and autobiographical images. Her photographs are published and exhibited frequently, most recently in the Focus Gallery in San Francisco, the Il Diaframma Canon in Milan, Italy, and the Triton Museum of Art in Santa Clara, California. The Honolulu Academy of Arts will present an exhibit of her work in 1987. She is a recipient of a 1982 National Endowment for the Arts Photographer's Fellowship.*